TRACKING AN ASSASSIN!

NICKOLAS FLUX and the Assassination of Abraham Lincoln

BY Nel Yomtov

ILLUSTRATED BY
Amerigo Pinelli

CONSULTANT:
Richard Bell, PhD
Associate Professor of History
University of Maryland, College Park

CAPSTONE PRESS
a capstone imprint

Graphic Library is published by Capstone Press,
1710 Roe Crest Drive, North Mankato, Minnesota 56003
www.capstonepub.com

Library of Congress Cataloging-in-Publication Data
Yomtov, Nelson.
  Tracking an assassin! : Nickolas Flux and the assassination of Abraham
Lincoln / by Nel Yomtov ; illustrated by Amerigo Pinelli.
    pages cm.—(Graphic library. Nicholas Flux history chronicles)
  Includes bibliographical references and index.
  Summary: "In graphic novel format, follows the adventures of Nickolas Flux as he
travels back in time to the assassination of Abraham Lincoln and joins the hunt for John
Wilkes Booth"—Provided by publisher.
  ISBN 978-1-4914-0252-8 (library binding)
  ISBN 978-1-4914-0257-3 (paperback)
  ISBN 978-1-4914-0261-0 (e-Book PDF)
1. Lincoln, Abraham, 1809-1865—Assassination—Juvenile literature. 2. Lincoln,
Abraham, 1809-1865—Assassination—Comic books, strips, etc. 3. Booth, John Wilkes,
1838–1865—Juvenile literature. 4. Booth, John Wilkes, 1838–1865—Comic books,
strips, etc. 5. Assassins—United States—Biography—Juvenile literature. 6. Assas-
sins—United States—Biography—Comic books, strips, etc. 7. Graphic novels. I. Pinelli,
Amerigo, illustrator. II. Title.
  E457.5.Y66 2015
  364.152'4092—dc23   2014003731

Photo Credits:
Design Elements: Shutterstock (backgrounds)

Editor's Note:
Direct quotations, noted in red type, appear on the following pages:

Pages 9, 10, 11, 12, 17, 24 (panel 1), and 27 from *Manhunt: The 12-Day Chase for Lincoln's Killer* by James L. Swanson (New York: Harper Perennial, 2007).

Page 24 (panel 2) from "Testimony of Sergt. Boston Corbett" *New York Times* (http://
www.nytimes.com/1865/05/18/news/testimony-of-sergt-boston-corbett.html

Page 29 from "The Gettysburg Address" by Abraham Lincoln, Abraham Lincoln Online
(http://www.abrahamlincolnonline.org/lincoln/speeches/gettysburg.htm).

EDITOR
Christopher L. Harbo

ART DIRECTOR
Nathan Gassman

DESIGNER
Ashlee Suker

PRODUCTION SPECIALIST
Jennifer Walker

COVER ARTIST
Dante Ginevra

Printed in the United States of America in Stevens Point, Wisconsin.

TABLE OF CONTENTS

CHAPTER ONE
BACKSTAGE JITTERS

Sparta Hills High School theater, backstage

Quiet, everyone. The curtain is about to go up.

Are the actors ready?

Yes, Ms. Park.

Take your places, please.

Are the props ready, Nick?

Everything is a-OK, Ms. Park.

My scenery is in position too.

This is so cool, Anne. I'm glad we volunteered to help out.

But I'm so nervous, Nick. What if something goes wrong?

Nah! What could go wrong?

I'm going to take a peek at the audience.

Wow! A full house!

Nick! Nick!

You forgot my stovepipe hat!

Oh, no! Wait here. I'll go get it!

Hurry! The curtain is going up any second!

I hope I'm not too late ...

FZZZT!

7

Washington, D.C., April 14, 1865, five days after the end of the Civil War

To your places, actors! The next scene will start soon!

Let's put on a good show for our special guest in the audience!

Backstage again! But where have I been zapped to this time?

Hmm, interesting.

KA-BLAMM!

Huh?

Sic semper tyrannis!*

*Latin for, "Thus always to tyrants!"

Ford's Theatre. A man jumping onto the stage.

Oh no! It can't be—I I've got to stop him!

Away from me, scoundrel!

Unnhff!

FWIK

FLUX FACT

Booth was a famous actor and well known at Ford's Theatre. He knew the play being performed that night. He fired his shot during a scene he knew would make the audience laugh to muffle the sound.

CHAPTER THREE
"HIS WOUND IS MORTAL"

Moments later ...

Is he dead, Dr. Leale? Can he recover? Oh, my dear husband.

I'll do all I can for him, Mrs. Lincoln. Clara Harris will stay with you while I tend to the president.

I raced up here as quickly as I could. I hope I can help in some way.

His wound is mortal. It is impossible for him to recover.

Oh, no!

We should take him to the White House.

Impossible. He'll never survive the trip.

FLUX FACT

Dr. Charles Leale was a surgeon in the Union Army during the Civil War. He was in the audience the night of the shooting. He was the first of several doctors to arrive in the presidential box.

14

FLUX FACT
Secretary of War Edwin Stanton served under Lincoln during the Civil War. He organized the Union's war efforts and helped guide the Union to victory.

75

From what the witnesses have told us, Booth is staying at the National Hotel nearby. Maybe there is evidence in his room.

I'll send investigators to have a look.

In the meantime, have the telegraph operators inform my officers in the region to look for Booth.

Booth supported the Confederate cause against our government. He may be fleeing south.

April 15, 5:00 a.m.

Ah, you're back, Nick. Any word on the hunt for Booth?

I saw Lieutenant Dana with his cavalry patrol on their way out of Washington. He said Booth is headed for the deep South but has to pass through Maryland first.

We must find him before he gets too far.

How is the president?

It doesn't look good, son.

FLUX FACT

A letter written by someone named "Sam" was found in Booth's room at the National Hotel. It led investigators to believe that many people—not only Booth—were involved in the plot to assassinate Lincoln.

April 24, morning

We've just received a telegram from the War Department. Two men were seen crossing the Potomac River from Maryland into Virginia on April 16!

Lieutenant Edward Doherty here in Washington will take charge of the search.

If those men are Booth and Herold, then the assassins have been in Virginia for the past eight days!

Report to Lieutenant Doherty. I want you to take down any testimony those killers give.

Yes, sir!

Finally! I'm in the hunt for President Lincoln's killers!

FLUX FACT

Two men had been seen crossing the Potomac River on April 16. It turned out they weren't John Wilkes Booth and David Herold. But the false alarm helped put the authorities on Booth's trail.

19

April 25, 4:00 p.m., Port Conway, Virginia

Have you seen these men, Mr. Rollins?

I'm not telling you anything. I have no love for the Union.

You'll answer my questions—or be arrested.

Since you put it that way ...

One of the men was hobbling.

That must be Booth. He broke his leg jumping to the stage at Ford's Theatre.

Any idea where they were headed?

How should I know? But they traveled with three Confederate soldiers. One of the soldiers is staying in Bowling Green, Virginia.

Get your horse, Rollins. You're taking us there.

It will take two hours to move our men across the river by ferry.

I'll help the troops get ready, Detective Baker.

FLUX FACT

William Rollins fought for the Confederacy during the Civil War. He was not eager to help the Union soldiers on their manhunt. Detective Baker's threat to arrest him changed Rollins' mind.

21

April 26, 12:30 a.m.

Lead us straight to the Garrett farm, soldier. And don't try any tricks.

If you do, it will be your death.

April 26, 2:00 a.m.

Surround the barn!

Stay close to me, Nick. This might get dangerous.

You bet, Detective Baker.

FLUX FACT

When the soldiers arrived at the farm, the Garrett family refused to tell them where Booth was hiding. John Garrett, a son of the farm's owner, revealed Booth's location only when Lieutenant Doherty threatened to shoot him.

KRACK!

FZZZZT!

Lay him here.

Tell mother, I die for my country.

Let him rest for a moment. Then we'll move him to the farmhouse porch.

27

MAJOR HENRY RATHBONE

Major Henry Rathbone struggled with Booth on the balcony of Ford's Theatre. He served in the Union Army during the Civil War (1861-1865) and was Lincoln's close friend. During the scuffle Booth slashed Rathbone's arm with his dagger.

END OF THE CIVIL WAR

The Confederacy surrendered to the Union on April 9, 1865, only five days before Booth assassinated Lincoln. The surrender marked the end of the Civil War, but there were still occasional fights between Confederate forces and Union troops, especially in the South. The hunt for Booth became more dangerous as U.S. troops moved farther south through Maryland and into Virginia.

BOOTH'S CONFEDERATE LOYALTIES

Although Booth did not fight in the Civil War, he supported the Confederacy. He strongly opposed the abolition of slavery in the United States and hated Lincoln with a passion.

PLANNING THE ASSASSINATION

On the morning of April 14, Booth learned that Mr. and Mrs. Lincoln would be attending the play *Our American Cousin* at Ford's Theatre that night. He immediately made plans for the assassination. He told several accomplices of his plan and assigned them the job of killing Secretary of State William Seward and Vice President Andrew Johnson. He also planned his escape route out of Washington.

KIDNAPPING PLOT

Booth's original plan was to kidnap Lincoln. He hoped to exchange him for Confederate soldiers held in Union prison camps. Booth had learned Lincoln would be attending a play just outside Washington, D. C., on March 17, 1865. He and his accomplices plotted to overtake the president's carriage on the way there. But Lincoln changed his plans at the last minute and never went to the play. Booth abandoned his kidnapping plot.

BOOTH'S ACCOMPLICES

Many of Booth's suspected accomplices were captured and jailed. Eventually eight suspects were put on trial. All were found guilty on June 30, 1865. David Herold, Lewis Powell, George Atzerodt, and Mary Surratt were hanged. Atzerodt had planned to kill Vice President Johnson, but didn't carry out the attack. Mary Surratt had provided shelter for Booth and his accomplices. Samuel Arnold, Dr. Samuel Mudd, and Michael O'Laughlen received prison terms. Each were part of the kidnapping plot. Dr. Mudd also tended to Booth's broken leg. Edwin Spangler, who helped Booth escape from Ford's Theatre, also went to prison.

GLOSSARY

ABOLITION (ab-uh-LISH-uhn) – the immediate end of something, such as slavery

ACCOMPLICE (uh-KAHM-plis) – someone who helps another person commit a crime

ASSASSINATION (uh-sass-uh-NAY-shun) – the murder of someone who is well known or important

CONFEDERACY (kuhn-FE-druh-see) – the Southern states that fought against the Northern states in the Civil War; also called the Confederate States of America

CONSPIRATOR (kuhn-SPIR-uh-tor) – a plotter; someone who takes part in a conspiracy

REBEL (REB-uhl) – someone who fights against a government or the people in charge of something

TELEGRAPH (TEL-uh-graf) – a machine that uses electronic signals to send messages over long distances

TESTIMONY (TES-tuh-moh-nee) – evidence given by a witness in a trial

TYRANT (TYE-ruhnt) – someone who rules other people in a cruel or unjust way

UNION (YOON-yuhn) – the United States of America; also the Northern states that fought against the Southern states in the Civil War

VOLUNTEER (vol-uhn-TIHR) – people who offer to do a job, usually without pay

READ MORE

HALLY, ASHLEIGH. *Abraham Lincoln.* American Heroes. Hamilton, Ga.: State Standards Pub., 2012.

KEATING, FRANK. *Abraham.* A Paula Wiseman Book. New York: Simon & Schuster Books for Young Readers, 2015.

MARA, WIL. *Abraham Lincoln.* Rookie Biographies. New York: Children's Press, 2014.

SCHOTT, JANE A. *How Did Abraham Lincoln Make History?* Sterling History Maker Revisions. Minneapolis: Sandy Creek, 2014.

INTERNET SITES

FactHound offers a safe, fun way to find Internet sites related to this book. All sites on FactHound have been researched by our staff.

Here's all you do:

Visit *www.facthound.com*

Type in this code: 9781476502528

Super-cool stuff! Check out projects, games and lots more at **www.capstonekids.com**

ABOUT THE AUTHOR

Nel Yomtov is a writer of children's nonfiction books and graphic novels. He specializes in writing about history, country studies, science, and biography. Nel has written frequently for Capstone, including other Nickolas Flux adventures such as *Defend Until Death!: Nickolas Flux and the Battle of the Alamo; Night of Rebellion!: Nickolas Flux and the Boston Tea Party;* and *Peril in Pompeii!: Nickolas Flux and the Eruption of Mount Vesuvius.* His graphic novel adaptation, *Jason and the Golden Fleece,* published by Stone Arch Books, was a winner of the 2009 Moonbeam Children's Book Award and the 2011 Lighthouse Literature Award. Nel lives in the New York City area.